Police Cars

by Marcia S. Freeman

Consulting Editor:
Gail Saunders-Smith, Ph.D.

Consultant:
Louis Mayo, Ph.D.
Executive Director
American Police Association

Pebble Books

an Imprint of Capstone Press
Mankato, Minnesota

Pebble Books are published by Capstone Press
818 North Willow Street, Mankato, Minnesota 56001
http://www.capstone-press.com

Library of Congress Cataloging-in-Publication Data
Freeman, Marcia S. (Marcia Sheehan), 1937–
    Police cars/by Marcia S. Freeman.
    p. cm.—(Community vehicles)
    Includes bibliographical references and index.
    Summary: Describes and illustrates police cars and the equipment they carry.
    ISBN 0-7368-0103-0
    1. Police vehicles—Juvenile literature. 2. Police—Equipment and supplies—
Juvenile literature. [1. Police vehicles. 2. Police—Equipment and supplies.]
I. Title. II. Series.
HV7936.V4F74 1999
629.2'088'3632—dc21

                                                                                    98-7056
                                                                                        CIP
                                                                                         AC

Note to Parents and Teachers

This series supports national social studies standards related to authority and government. This book describes and illustrates police cars and the equipment they carry. The photographs support early readers in understanding the text. The sentence structures offer subtle challenges. This book introduces early readers to vocabulary used in this subject area. The vocabulary is defined in the Words to Know section. Early readers may need assistance in reading some words and in using the Table of Contents, Words to Know, Read More, Internet Sites, and Index/Word List sections of the book.

2

Table of Contents

4

Police cars help police officers do their jobs. Police cars help officers keep people safe.

Police cars have sirens.
Police cars have flashing
lights. Police cars use sirens
and lights to travel to
emergencies fast.

alley light

Police cars have alley lights. Alley lights help police officers work at night. Alley lights light up large areas.

Police cars carry supplies in their trunks. Trunks hold first-aid kits to help people who are hurt. Trunks hold fire extinguishers to put out small fires.

Police cars have two-way radios. Police officers talk to dispatchers on two-way radios. Dispatchers send police officers to emergencies.

Police cars carry small computers. Police officers use computers to report on their work.

Police cars carry flashlights. The flashlights have bright lights. Police officers use the flashlights to see in dark places.

18

Police cars carry radar guns. Radar guns show how fast cars are going. Police officers stop drivers who are going too fast.

Some police cars carry police dogs. Police dogs help police officers do their jobs. Police dogs ride in the back of police cars.

Words to Know

alley lights—bright lights on police cars; alley lights light up large areas and help police officers see numbers on houses.

emergency—a time of danger; people should dial 911 for help during an emergency.

fire extinguisher—a holder with water or chemicals inside it; people use fire extinguishers to put out fires.

radar gun—a machine that shows how fast something is going; police officers use radar guns to measure how fast cars go.

siren—a machine that makes a loud sound

trunk—a space in the back of a car; police officers keep supplies in the trunks of police cars.

Read More

Ready, Dee. *Police Officers.* Community Helpers. Mankato, Minn.: Bridgestone Books, 1997.

Somerville, Louisa. *Rescue Vehicles.* Look Inside Cross-Sections. New York: Dorling Kindersley, 1995.

Winkleman, Katherine K. *Police Patrol.* New York: Walker and Co., 1996.

Internet Sites

Cop Cruisers
http://copcruisers.simplenet.com/index3.html

Police Car Web Site
http://www.op.net/~rwcar4/police.htm

The Police K-9 Page
http://www.k9cop.com

Index/Word List

Word Count: 177
Early-Intervention Level: 11

Editorial Credits
Colleen Sexton, editor; Clay Schotzko/Icon Productions, cover designer;
    Sheri Gosewisch, photo researcher

Photo Credits
Barbara J. Coxe, 20
Bruce Cotler/911 Pictures, 1
Leslie O'Shaughnessy, 4, 8, 16, 18
Mike Heller/911 Pictures, 6, 10, 12
Photo Network/Mark Sherman, cover
Shaffer Photography/James L. Shaffer, 14